Spiritual Works of Mercy

by
Mgr Paul Grogan

*All booklets are published thanks to the
generous support of the members of the
Catholic Truth Society*

CATHOLIC TRUTH SOCIETY
PUBLISHERS TO THE HOLY SEE

Contents

Introduction 3

1. Counsel the doubtful 8

2. Instruct the ignorant 15

3. Admonish the sinner 22

4. Comfort the afflicted 29

5. Forgive offences 36

6. Bear wrongs patiently 43

7. Pray for the living and the dead 50

All rights reserved. First published 2015 by The Incorporated Catholic Truth Society, 40-46 Harleyford Road London SE11 5AY Tel: 020 7640 0042 Fax: 020 7640 0046. © 2015 The Incorporated Catholic Truth Society.

ISBN 978 1 78469 087 8

Introduction

A student at the university where I used to be Chaplain was deeply unsettled. She felt drawn to Christianity and tried visiting a number of churches but left them dissatisfied and disoriented. Then one evening she found herself talking to a friend, another student who had converted to Catholicism, as they prepared to go to the university bar. She mentioned her dilemma and the other student began very naturally to explain what it was that attracted her to the Catholic faith. The conversation went on for two hours and they just reached the bar for "last orders". A few days afterwards, the first young woman came to me for instruction in the faith. She was extraordinarily resolved, clear-sighted and receptive of Church teaching. It was a joy to receive her into the Catholic Church some months later.

During that precious two-hour conversation, one student undertook a spiritual work of mercy with regard to her friend. She enlightened her about the beauty of the Catholic faith. In this way she was, to use the traditional terminology, "instructing the ignorant". She rescued her friend from the unhappiness of confusion and indecision.

Most Catholics I know want to live their faith more completely. Many feel a little perplexed about how they might go about this. That is why it is so good that the

Church is currently focusing particularly on the corporal and spiritual works of mercy. As Pope Francis has written, Jesus introduces us to these works of mercy in his preaching so that we can know whether or not we are living as his disciples (*Misericordiae Vultus*, 15).

Acts of Mercy

There are seven spiritual works of mercy just as there are seven corporal works of mercy (please see Mgr Richard Atherton's companion CTS booklet on the latter). The number is significant. In the Judeo-Christian imagination seven symbolises completeness. These acts of mercy are a means by which disciples of Jesus can make a whole-life response to God's goodness towards them. While some members of the Church may be especially well placed to perform a particular work, all members of the Church have opportunities to engage in each work in different ways.

The spiritual works of mercy are: counsel the doubtful; instruct the ignorant; admonish sinners; comfort the afflicted; forgive offences; bear wrongs patiently; and pray for the living and the dead. We can see immediately that the term "spiritual" is here used in a wide sense encompassing the whole of the interior life. We can also see certain connections between some of the works. For example, counselling the doubtful and instructing the ignorant both involve helping people to come to a greater knowledge of the faith while forgiving offences makes us readier to bear wrongs patiently. Within the Catholic tradition, the spiritual works have been judged to have a higher priority than the corporal works precisely because they concern the interior life.

The key to understanding the spiritual works of mercy is to recognise that they are in the first instance *God's* acts of mercy. Those who engage in them are the human agents who make it possible for God to reach out and alleviate people's unhappiness. Members of the Church are minded to co-operate in this way because they know that God has shown his mercy to them first (*Misericordiae Vultus*, 9).

What is mercy?

The word "mercy" needs explaining. In common parlance it denotes the decision of a powerful person not to punish another. This is clearly not what mercy means with respect to God the Father of Jesus Christ! Our English word is a translation of the Latin "misericordia" which can best be translated as "the heart that shares another's misery". The spiritual acts of mercy reveal the Father's heart yearning to give solace to his beloved sons and daughters. The Father's love for us is so great that he who is all-powerful has bound himself to us through the Covenant of Christ's death and resurrection. He cannot now withdraw his favour from us if he is to remain true to himself.

Jesus Christ is "the face of the Father's mercy" (*MV*, 1). The spiritual works of mercy have an inner coherence because each is drawn from the life of Jesus. Indeed, we may say that Jesus continues to act through these works undertaken by his disciples because he is the Head of the Body of which they are the members (cf. *Col* 1:18).

In performing spiritual works of mercy his disciples are transformed. They become more human because they become more Christ-like. Each work involves a movement from self to others. In the corporal works of mercy this movement is visible. In the spiritual works of mercy the movement is sometimes invisible but the self-sacrificial love required is the same, if not greater. I strive, for example, unbeknown to the person who annoys me, to leave behind my sense of resentment and focus on that person's good qualities. Or I postpone doing something which is congenial to me and devote myself to praying for others who may well be unaware of the benefit that my intercession on their behalf is conferring upon them.

Mercy and the community

The performance of spiritual works of mercy also transforms communities. Each community, including the Church, is a network of relationships. The healthier these relationships are, the more the community thrives. By, for example, gently inviting somebody to desist from objectionable behaviour I am acting to reduce the strain which that person's actions are causing others. By comforting somebody who is afflicted I am rescuing that person from isolation.

What happens through the spiritual works of mercy, then, is this: working through the interior life of his sons and daughters, God the Father applies his mercy, made visible in Jesus Christ, to different difficult human situations and assuages distress. In the process, those who co-operate with the Father's will are inwardly transformed and the communities in which they participate, including their local Church community, are built up.

Here we see how important the spiritual works of mercy are in terms of evangelisation. When somebody takes an interest in us in a charitable, non-possessive way we feel affirmed and ready to respond. Moreover, all of us want to participate in open, life-giving communities. The more the Church becomes a vibrant, united family whose members seek the good of others, including those outside her visible boundaries, the more attractive will be the gospel she proclaims.

I will situate each work in terms of scripture, Christ and the practice of the Church, describe its nature and goodness and suggest a few ways in which we can perform it today. I will also note how each work is exemplified by a passage in European literature, greatly shaped as that has been historically by Christian culture. I will also draw a connection between each of the seven spiritual works of mercy and one of the seven sacraments in the belief that, ordered to human flourishing as both the works and the sacraments are, the latter can be illuminative of the former.

1. Counsel the doubtful

There are two types of doubtfulness. The first resides at the level of affectivity: I experience an emotional blockage which prevents me from truly receiving the good news that God the Father is all-merciful and that his heart, manifested in the Sacred Heart of Jesus, longs beyond all knowing for me to enter into communion with him. The second resides at the level of the intellect: I cannot accept that a loving God exists given the suffering in the world and the apparent absurdity of all human existence. In practice, intellectual objections to Christianity are often accompanied by affective issues as well: resistance to the truth claims of the Church is made stronger by a perhaps unnamed fear of personal surrender to God the Father which faith, were it to be embraced, would entail.

Origin in Scripture

We might say that the Bible is an extended narration of how successive figures sent by God intervened in the lives of the people whom he had created and had called to live in his presence to assure them of his good purposes towards them. It is extraordinary how quickly those whom God had helped lost faith in him. We might think for example of the Israelites whom God had saved from the pursuing

Egyptians and who then opted to worship a golden calf of their own creation (*Ex* 32). The authors of Judges, 1 and 2 Chronicles, 1 and 2 Samuel and 1 and 2 Kings use fidelity to the Covenant as the sole frame of reference for determining the goodness or not of a particular ruler. Successive prophets, including Isaiah and Jeremiah, exhorted rulers and the people accordingly.

The subsequent disasters of first the fall of the northern Kingdom of Israel in the seventh century BC and then the fall of Jerusalem and the exile in Babylon in the sixth century BC were interpreted as God's punishment on the people who had, practically speaking, rejected him. Now doubtfulness was expressed differently. The question was no longer, "Will the Lord God of Israel really protect us?" and became instead, "If the Lord God of Israel does indeed love us, how can he have allowed these catastrophes to have occurred?" From this shift in questioning emerged a new and stronger faith which was articulated by the later Isaiah and in the Book of Daniel, among others. Drawing on God's goodness in the past, such writers looked forward to God's intervention at the end of time. The Jews took courage from that prospect to face the challenges of the present.

The Jewish liturgical feasts were invaluable in this process of remembrance. For example, the words of Moses, beginning, "Hear, O Israel: the Lord our God is the one Lord," were and are read out on each Sabbath. Moses urged the people to love the Lord God with all their heart, all their soul and all their strength and to teach their children about him. He added: "take care you do not forget the Lord your God who brought you out of the land of Egypt" (*Dt* 6:4-13). The Psalms, which were used in Temple worship and in the synagogues, also repeatedly recall God's faithfulness to the Covenant. For example, the Psalmist declares, "Come consider the works of the Lord/ the redoubtable deeds he has done on the earth" (*Ps* 45:8).

Example of Christ

When the glorified and risen Jesus stands before Thomas after his resurrection on the eighth day, the day of the celebration of the Eucharist, and invites him to doubt no longer but to believe, the moment marks the high point of the practice of counselling the doubtful which stretches back centuries within the Judaic tradition (*Jn* 20:24-29). The moment also looks forwards to those who in subsequent centuries, like our own, would find faith problematic. Jesus directs Thomas's attention to the wounds in his hands and to the wound in his side. In Jesus God has taken into himself all human suffering. He has done this because his love for us, expressed through Jesus's Sacred Heart, is immeasurably great.

We can understand the encounter between Jesus and Thomas more fully when we see it in the context of some of Jesus's other sayings and actions. "Of course I want to! Be cured!" he told the leper, revealing his deep-seated desire to rescue his beloved people from oppression (*Mt* 8:2-3). "How is it that you have no faith?" he asked his apostles after he had calmed the storm (*Mk* 4:40). Then, when they asked him to increase their faith, he said, "Were your faith the size of a mustard seed you could say to this mulberry tree, 'Be uprooted and planted in the sea' and it would obey you" (*Lk* 17:5-6). Jesus repeatedly seeks to persuade his disciples to entrust themselves to him always more completely.

Example of Christians historically

The early Church took upon itself with vim the task of counselling the doubtful. The key account is that of St Paul speaking at the Council of the Areopagus in Athens when he skilfully drew a connection between "An Unknown God", to whom he had seen an altar dedication in the city, and the one God who had raised Jesus from the dead (*Ac* 17:16-34). Paul also revealed, through his dazzling rhetorical skills in a passage in the Letter to the Romans, what it feels like to be the object of God's importunate love, beginning: "Nothing therefore can come between us and the love of Christ…" (*Rm* 8:31-39).

Later interventions by the Church to counsel those who were doubtful show a similar Spirit-filled confidence and gentleness. We can think of St Dominic in the thirteenth century who, to rescue people from a false understanding of God held by the Cathars (who believed that all matter was evil and who therefore denied the Incarnation), sent out his followers to live simply among the people with a single aim, namely to preach the truth. We can also think of Pope St John Paul II in the last century recognising that the time had come to put all the energies of the Church into a "new evangelisation" of society.

The nature and goodness of counselling the doubtful

1. We always come to truth together. The word "counsel" is connected with "council", a group of people who are engaged in a common enterprise. Counselling the doubtful involves witnessing to personal faith and recalling God's mercies of the past as these have been personally experienced.

2. Doubt is an ordinary aspect of a life of faith, a painful moment which others can help us to move beyond and which affords us an opportunity to surrender more whole-heartedly to God.

3. The members of the Church are in constant need of being evangelised themselves if they are to evangelise others (Blessed Paul VI, *Evangelii Nuntiandi*, 15).

4. Liturgical celebrations constitute an important moment of counselling the doubtful: through participating in them we remember our identity before God.

5. Counselling the doubtful is a response to a universal human desire, expressed or unexpressed, namely to discover meaning in life through faith in God.

What can you do practically speaking?

1. Go to Mass and consciously open your heart to the Holy Spirit who can remind you of God's mercy celebrated in the Eucharist.

2. Consider finding a spiritual director who can help you to go deeper in your faith.

3. At the parish level, encourage those whose faith may be weak, e.g. establish a faith group for parents of children who are receiving first sacraments.

4. Dialogue about the Christian faith respectfully and purposefully on occasion with non-Christian friends or colleagues as circumstances allow.

Prayer in support

Searching for God by St Anselm of Canterbury
(1033-1109)

O Lord, my God, teach my heart this day where and how to see you, where and how to find you. You have made me and remade me, and you have bestowed on me all the good things I possess, and still I do not know you. I have not yet done that for which I was made. Teach me to seek you, for I cannot seek you unless you teach me, or find you unless you show yourself to me. Let me seek you in my desire; let me desire you in my seeking. Let me find you by loving you; let me love you when I find you.

Literature

The seventeenth century poet George Herbert exquisitely
captures our reluctance to accept the truth of God's mercy
towards us in the poem *Love* which begins with the line:
"Love bade me welcome; yet my soul drew back,/Guilty of
dust and sin." Love, or Christ, gently helps the poet to move
beyond his sense of unworthiness. "'You must sit down',
says Love, 'and taste my meat.'/So I did sit and eat."

Sacrament

In Baptism we become sons and daughters of our Father in
heaven. Counselling the doubtful is fundamentally about
reminding people of their identity before God.

2. Instruct the ignorant

The emphasis in the first spiritual work of mercy is on accompanying people in their search for God. The emphasis in the second one is on equipping them to engage in this journey of faith.

Origins in Scripture

In the Old Testament, God is the teacher *par excellence*. He delivers the Ten Commandments to Moses (*Ex* 20:1-7) and enjoins him to communicate other related precepts to his people (*Ex* 20:22-23:33). God wishes to show his people ways in which they can live in his presence which will honour the Covenant that he is establishing with them (*Ex* 24:1-11). If they comply they will receive his blessings.

Centuries later, when the Israelites returned to the ruins of Jerusalem from their exile in Babylon, they asked Ezra the scribe "to bring the Book of the Law of Moses which the Lord God prescribed for Israel." He gathered them before the Water Gate and read from the Book "from early morning til noon"; all the people "listened attentively" and Ezra translated and gave the sense of the Law "so that the people understood what was read". At the end "they were all in tears" and Ezra had to bid them rejoice, which they subsequently did because "they had understood the meaning of what had been proclaimed to them" (*Ne* 8:1-12).

Alongside the great teaching of the Law, there is the Wisdom tradition, which is an extended reflection on human experience comprising several books in the Bible. It was based on the premise that through engaging with reality we discover God. The Psalms form part of this tradition. The Psalmist declares: "The heavens proclaim the glory of God/and the firmament shows forth the work of his hands" (*Ps* 18:1).

All people, believers and non-believers, long to reach "the deep waters" of knowledge (*Pr* 20:5). Knowledge is not something that is merely desirable; it is essential: Wisdom, personified, declares "he who finds me finds life" (*Pr* 8:35). Knowledge can be obtained simply through the use of human reason but, according to this tradition, searchers for truth are able to grasp things more easily "within the horizon of faith" (Pope St John Paul II, *Fides et Ratio*, 16).

Example of Christ

In the New Testament Christ is the consummate teacher. The Gospels frequently mention that he is engaging in this activity. In Luke's Gospel, he begins his teaching right at the beginning of his public ministry: "He taught in their synagogues and everyone praised him" (*Lk* 4:15). Matthew describes how Jesus "went up the hill" to deliver the Beatitudes (*Mt* 5:1): the hill recalls Mount Sinai; the

Beatitudes are the Commandments of the New Covenant which Jesus is to establish through his death and resurrection.

Jesus appoints his apostles as teachers. In John's Gospel, he assures them: "…the Holy Spirit, whom the Father will send in my name, will teach you everything and remind you of all I have said to you" (*Jn* 14:26). At the end of Matthew's Gospel, Jesus tells them: "Go, therefore, make disciples of all the nations; baptise them in the name of the Father and of the Son and of the Holy Spirit, and teach them to observe all the commands I gave you. And know that I am with you always; yes, to the end of time" (*Mt* 28:19-20). This teaching is concerned not merely with doctrine but also with morals: the apostles are to speak about Jesus's "commandments", for example, "Love one another, as I have loved you" (*Jn* 15:12). The reference to baptising shows that the moral teaching is not about how one should live generally speaking but rather about how one should live as a member of the Church. The apostles will be real teachers, using their particular gifts and knowledge of their Risen Lord, but Jesus will also continue to teach *through* them: he will be with the apostles and the Church "always".

Example of Christians historically

The early Christians were devoted to "the teaching of the apostles" (*Ac* 2:42). It was quickly understood that there was a body of "sound teaching" (*2 Tm* 4:3) with which the apostles had been entrusted. They were to share the truths of the faith as widely as possible: if people did not hear about them, they could not believe (*Rm* 10:14-17). On some occasions teaching was directed at a large crowd, such as when Peter spoke at Pentecost (*Ac* 2:14-41); at other times there were moments of one-to-one instruction, such as when Philip catechised the eunuch and then baptised him (*Ac* 8:26-40).

Throughout each era the Church has responded to people's need of education. The monastic movement, which began in the early centuries, has always prioritised learning. The Jesuits, who were founded by St Ignatius of Loyola in the sixteenth century, responded to the Protestant Reformation by committing themselves to explaining the truths of the Catholic faith systematically.

In the nineteenth century two great Catholic education-alists emerged: St John Bosco in Turin and Blessed John Henry Newman in Britain. Don Bosco, who established the Salesian Order, concentrated on poor uneducated boys in his city; he devised "the preventive system". He wrote: "These young people have real need of some kind person who will care for them, work with them, guide them in virtue, keep them away from evil…" His catecheses were always short so that the boys would not become bored.

Blessed John Henry Newman helped set up the Catholic University of Ireland in Dublin. He stressed the importance of the "personal influence" which tutors in a university could have on their students: "the young for the most part cannot be driven but on the other hand, are open to persuasion and to the influence of kindness and personal attachment," he wrote. He also established the Oratory School in Birmingham. He would not accept that reflecting on the Christian faith could be separated from other intellectual enquiry: "Because reality is a single, undivided whole and because the object of knowledge is truth as such, all knowledge forms one large system or complex fact." He saw the job of education as seeking "to fit men for this world while training them for another."

In the last century, the publication of *The Catechism of the Catholic Church* was a remarkable event. A summary of the teachings of the Second Vatican Council, this four-part volume was a response to what St John Paul II described as Catholics' "right to sound catechesis" (*Catechesi Tradendae*, 14). Pope Emeritus Benedict noted in his Preface to the version aimed at young people, *YouCat*, that today's young people "need to be more deeply rooted in the faith" than the generation of their parents if they are to face the challenges of modernity.

The nature and goodness of this work of mercy

1. Through instruction, I "build up" a person (the Latin word *"instruere"* means "construct") and I make them freer.

2. Instruction involves handing on to the next generation the patrimony of truth of the family of the Church.

3. Teaching is an exercise of self-sacrificial love and hence has a particular vocational quality.

4. In Catholic education all subjects are seen in the light of and are integrated with the faith: hence the teaching of any subject can be an exercise of this spiritual work of mercy.

What can you do practically speaking?

1. Accept the challenge of life-long learning as a Catholic. Seek out resources or groups in the parish or elsewhere (including on-line) for ongoing faith development.

2. If time allows, offer your services to contribute to others' faith development, whether children (in, for example, sacramental preparation) or adults (in, for example, an RCIA group).

3. Consider teaching as a career. There is a shortage of practising Catholic teachers.

4. If you are a priest, devote adequate time to homily preparation during the week, acknowledging that this is a priority, perhaps using resources suggested by the new Homiletic Directory.

Prayer in support

Prayer before study by St Thomas Aquinas (1225-1274)

Creator of all things, true Source of light and wisdom, lofty origin of all being, graciously let a ray of Your brilliance penetrate into the darkness of my understanding and take from me the double darkness in which I have been born, an obscurity of both sin and ignorance. Give me a sharp sense of understanding, a retentive memory, and the ability to grasp things correctly and fundamentally. Grant me the talent of being exact in my explanations, and the ability to express myself with thoroughness and charm. Point out the beginning, direct the progress, and help in completion; through Christ our Lord. Amen.

Literature

In Charles Dickens' *Hard Times*, Thomas Gradgrind, headmaster in Coketown, has a very narrow view of education: "Now, what I want is, Facts. Teach these boys and girls nothing but Facts. Facts alone are wanted in life. Plant nothing else, and root out everything else." During the course of the novel he comes to see the inadequacy of his utilitarian approach and to appreciate the need for education to feed the human spirit.

Sacrament

In the Sacrament of Confirmation we receive the Holy Spirit who leads us "to the complete truth" (*Jn* 16:13) and whose seven gifts to us include wisdom, understanding and knowledge.

3. Admonish the sinner

According to the Catholic tradition, sin is looking for happiness in places where it cannot be found. The third spiritual work of mercy is therefore linked to the second. It involves, in effect, helping a person to see his/her situation more clearly and providing the necessary support for the person to renounce harmful behaviour.

Origins in Scripture

The most dramatic moment of admonition in the Old Testament comes when the Prophet Nathan rebukes King David for having both committed adultery with Bathsheba and arranged for her husband, Uriah the Hittite, one of his army commanders, to be killed in battle (2 S 12: 1-15). Nathan skilfully draws the king towards a new self-awareness. He tells him a story about a rich man who owns many sheep but who, to feed a guest, kills the one sheep owned by a poor man. "The man who did this deserves to die!" David exclaims. "You are the man," Nathan retorts and then describes how, despite having many wives himself, David took Bathsheba. David replies: "I have sinned against the Lord God." The passage reveals how a man who is fundamentally good, like King David, needs help to accept that he has done wrong. Nathan, very respectfully, affords him the opportunity to apply his keenly felt sense of justice to his own situation so that he may experience the relief of declaring his guilt and hence emerge from the nightmare of continuing self-deception.

In this respect, Nathan is successfully communicating the gentleness and respectfulness of God. When, elsewhere in the Old Testament, the prophets lambast the people for failing to live according to the Covenant, they invariably indicate that the Lord God is very ready to relent, if only they would make some movement towards him. God finds it hard to understand that the Israelites should be so heedless of their own interests that they neglect their relationship with him. They have abandoned (God) "the fountain of living water, only to dig cisterns for themselves, leaky cisterns that hold no water" (*Jr* 2:13). God's admonitions could not be gentler: "'Come now, let us talk this over,' says the Lord God. 'Though yours sins are like scarlet, they shall be white as snow; though they are red as crimson, they shall be like wool'" (*Is* 1:18).

Example of Christ

Perhaps the most instructive example of admonition by Christ comes in his dialogue with the woman who was caught committing adultery (*Jn* 8:1-11). "'Woman, where are they? Has no one condemned you?' 'No one, sir', she replied. 'Neither do I condemn you,' said Jesus. 'Go away, and don't sin anymore.'" The men who wished to condemn the woman were seeking to identify her with her wrongful act, in part, no doubt, through prurience, and in part so that they could experience a sense of difference from her and so feel better about themselves. Jesus wishes merely to release her. The directness of Jesus's final words - "don't sin anymore" - is intended to reinforce the woman's awareness that adultery can bring her only unhappiness (in itself, that is, regardless of the attitude of others): it expresses Jesus's respect for her as one who is capable of conversion.

Jesus enjoins his followers to adopt his sensitive approach towards those who sin. He says: "If your brother does something wrong, go and have it out with him alone, between your two selves" (*Mt* 18:15). The phrase "alone, between your two selves" emphasises both the privacy of the interchange - necessary for the preservation of a person's reputation - and the fact that this is an interpersonal encounter: it is an act of accompaniment. Only if this does not work is a person to "take one or two others along" to admonish the wrongdoer and, if that does not work, to "report it to the community", i.e. the local Church.

Example of Christians historically

A beautiful example of admonition in the early Church is that given by St Monica in regard to her husband, Patricius, as recounted by their son, St Augustine, in Book Nine of *The Confessions* in the fourth century AD. He writes:

"…when she had arrived at a marriageable age, she was given to a husband whom she served as her lord. And she busied herself to gain him to You, preaching You unto him by her behaviour; by which You made her fair, and reverently amiable, and admirable unto her husband. For she so bore the wronging of her bed as never to have any dissension with her husband on account of it. For she waited for Your mercy upon him, that by believing in You he might become chaste. And besides this, as he was earnest in friendship, so was he violent in anger; but she had learned that an angry husband should not be resisted, neither in deed, nor even in word. But so soon as he was grown calm and tranquil, and she saw a fitting moment, she would give him a reason for her conduct, should he have been excited without cause."

St Monica's sensitivity is remarkable. In a few short sentences we learn how she helped Patricius to build on the goodness she perceived in him (he was "earnest in friendship") by exercising different spiritual works of mercy towards him: she both forgave offences and she bore wrongs patiently. Most importantly, however, she admonished him, but only when she realised that he was in a correct frame of mind to benefit from her words. She was able to negotiate her way so adeptly through their relationship because she was confident that God would in time grant his mercy to her husband to rescue him from the behaviour that was making both him and her unhappy.

Her act was in keeping with a Christian tradition of admonition which St Paul had done much to foster. St Paul counselled caution and respect: "Brothers, if one of you misbehaves, the more spiritual of you who set him right should do so in a spirit of gentleness, not forgetting that you may be tempted yourselves" (*Ga* 6:1).

St Thomas Aquinas developed the tradition with his customary clarity. He noted that admonition is always something that an *individual* does; it is not something which the community engages in. It is done out of love. Hence it is not an act of authority: it has nothing to do with punishment. Given that it is an act of love anybody can and should exercise it. It must be done as privately as possible because "reputation is the greatest of the external goods." There is no point in trying to correct somebody who is not in a frame of mind to receive correction. (*Disputed Questions on the Virtues: On Brotherly Correction*)

The nature and goodness of this work of mercy

1. It is a response of love to the needs of the person who has erred, helping him/her to come to a fuller understanding of his/her situation at the moment when this person is capable of receiving this help and benefiting from it.

2. Effective admonition requires the person who is engaging in it to be humbly aware that he/she shares in a solidarity of sin with the person whom he/she is trying to

help. Hence it is likely that the one admonishing now will need in turn to be admonished.

3. Admonition is directed at a particular individual but the whole Church benefits indirectly because sin invariably causes disintegration within the community.

What can you do practically speaking?

1. Gently alert a friend to behaviour that will be harmful to him/her if you think your friend is able to listen.

2. Be prepared to benefit from others' admonition of you and to be thankful for their kindness.

3. Take seriously your responsibility, in charity, for encouraging and ensuring high standards at work.

Prayer in support

For fortitude and wisdom

Heavenly Father, who alone can judge sinners, give us the courage through your Holy Spirit, to speak words of truth to a brother or sister who has fallen into a sinful pattern of behaviour and who stands in need of our support. May the same Holy Spirit guide us to choose the right moment to speak, a moment when the other person is ready to benefit. May all we do be done in charity and humility and may we in our turn be always open to correction by others. Through Christ our Lord. Amen.

Literature

In Jane Austen's *Emma*, Mr Knightley cares deeply for the eponymous heroine, notwithstanding her immaturity. Emma publicly ridicules a disadvantaged older single lady in her social set by laughingly pointing out in a clever throwaway remark that she is garrulous. Mr Knightley chooses a moment privately to upbraid Emma who manages, after an interior struggle, to accept his criticism: her subsequent attempts to apologise to the woman forms the key to the whole novel.

Sacrament

We begin the celebration of the Sacrament of the Eucharist by repenting of our sinfulness and receiving absolution. In this way we respond to the prior admonition of the Holy Spirit who demonstrates respect for us, reminds us of our worth and enables to enter more completely into freedom.

4. Comfort the afflicted

There is a clear overlap between the third and the fourth spiritual works of mercy. We afflict ourselves because of our sinful behaviour and another person's admonition can bring us comfort in the midst of the pain of personal conversion. At the same time, many of our afflictions are not the results of our wrong acts: they simply reflect the fact that we are living in a fallen world. They include invisible but very significant problems such as loneliness, untold anxieties and a sense of alienation.

Origins in Scripture

In the Old Testament, God is attentive to his people's needs. From the burning bush, he tells Moses: "I have seen the miserable state of my people in Egypt. I have heard their appeal to be free of their slave-drivers. Yes, I am well aware of their sufferings" (*Ex* 3:7). Having noticed their affliction God frees them from the Egyptians and leads them through the Red Sea and the wilderness to the Promised Land so that they may experience peace and prosperity.

Centuries later, the Lord God, speaking through the Prophet Isaiah in the Book of Consolation (*Is* 40-55), which was written, we understand, at the end of the sixth century BC, promises a new exodus (*Is* 41:17-20). This exodus could refer to the journey that the Jewish exiles took from Babylon to Jerusalem at about this time. It also resonates with the hope that God is going to intervene at the end of time and take his suffering people to himself.

The Book begins with the Lord God addressing the Prophet: "'Console my people, console them,' says your God. 'Speak to the heart of Jerusalem and call to her that her time of service is ended, her sin is atoned for…'" (*Is* 40:1-2). The Book describes why the people should take heart. Most importantly, God declares simply that he is *with them*: "For I, the Lord your God, I am holding you by the right hand; I tell you, 'Do not be afraid, I will help you'" (*Is* 41:13). Moreover, God reminds his people that he is all-powerful: "I it was who made the earth, and created man who is on it. I it was who spread out the heavens with my hands…" (*Is* 45:12).

God is to send the people his servant, "my chosen one in whom my soul delights" (*Is* 42:1). The servant will bring God's comfort to everybody. Addressing the servant, God says: "I will make you the light of the nations so that my salvation may reach to the ends of the earth" (*Is* 49:6). Mysteriously this salvation is to come about through the ill treatment of the servant: "By his sufferings shall my servant justify many, taking their faults on himself" (*Is* 53:11).

Example of Christ

God's assurances in Isaiah that he is with his people are fulfilled in Jesus, who is Emmanuel, "God with us" (*Mt* 1:23). Jesus declares at the outset of his public ministry that he has come "to set the downtrodden free" (*Lk* 4:18). He has an eye for those who are distressed: "And when he saw the crowds he felt sorry for them because they were harassed and dejected, like sheep without a shepherd" (*Mt* 9:36).

He seeks out people who are on the margins of society and spends time with them: we may think for example of the meal that he has with the tax collectors and sinners following St Matthew's conversion (*Mt* 9:10) or the day he visited Zacchaeus (*Lk* 19:1-10). He is also present to people who are experiencing different kinds of inner turmoil. We may think of the rich young man who ran up to him, knelt before him and asked "Good master, what must I do to inherit eternal life?" (*Mk* 10:17-22) Alternatively, there is the woman who came to him in the house of Simon the Pharisee and, weeping, kissed his feet and anointed them with ointment (*Lk* 7:36-38).

Jesus rebukes the scribes and Pharisees for failing to accept others' weaknesses through the overly exiguous way in which they interpret the Law. "They tie up heavy burdens and lay them on men's shoulders, but will they lift a finger to move them? Not they!" (*Mt* 23:4) Significantly, as Jesus notes, the scribes and Pharisees remain apart from the rest of the people, taking the place of honour at banquets or the front seats in the synagogues. By contrast, Jesus wants people to draw close to him. He says: "Come to me, all you who labour and are overburdened, and I will give you rest. Shoulder my yoke and learn from me, for I am gentle and humble in heart and you will find rest for your souls. Yes, my yoke is easy and my burden light" (*Mt* 11:28-30).

Jesus comforts those who are afflicted by entering into their brokenness and taking it upon himself. He whose burden is light shoulders the heavy burden of the cross. Then he allows his gentle heart to be pierced so that he may continue to comfort those who are afflicted through the sacraments of his holy Church which, according to the Fathers, came into existence at that moment: the blood and water flowing from Jesus's heart symbolise respectively Baptism and the Eucharist (*Jn* 19:34).

Example of Christians historically

Christians in the early centuries experienced a succession of persecutions in the Roman Empire. In the later part of the first century, the author of the Letter to the Hebrews comforted some of them by reminding them of their endurance to date, adding: "Only a little while now, a very little while, and the one that is coming will have come; he will not delay" (*Heb* 10:32-39). It is quite striking that in this period Christ's coming at the end of time is the Christians' principle comfort.

Other Christians struggled to understand how the resurrection of Jesus helped them as they grieved the loss of a loved one. St Paul instructs them in their ignorance: "We want you be quite certain, brothers, about those who have died, to make sure that you do not grieve about them, like the other people who have no hope." After explaining that we hope to rise with Christ, he writes: "So we shall stay with the Lord for ever." Again we see that the ultimate consolation is simply being with Christ.

A good modern example of somebody who lived this work of mercy heroically is Blessed Chiara Badano, who died of cancer in 1990, aged nineteen, and who was associated with the Focolare Movement. In her final months she devoted herself to encouraging those around her. For example, she spent time walking in the hospital grounds with another female patient who was suffering from depression, notwithstanding the fact that it cost her a great deal emotionally. One of the doctors at the hospital said, "Through her smile, and through her eyes full of light, she showed us that death doesn't exist; only life exists." A friend from the Focolare Movement said, "At first we thought we'd visit her to keep her spirits up, but very soon we understood that, in fact, we were the ones who needed her. Her life was like a magnet drawing us to her."

The nature and goodness of this work of mercy

1. It rescues people from the sense of isolation, which can often be a consequence of suffering.

2. It reminds people of their innate worth.

3. It helps people to become stronger in addressing underlying problems.

What can you do practically speaking?

1. Take the first move in reaching out to somebody who is interiorly suffering in a friendly, non-judgemental way.

2. Strive to be a person who is approachable. Seek to "be present" to those whom you meet. Then they will feel confident in sharing their problems with you when the time comes.

3. Be ready to encourage people who have particular needs to connect with appropriate professionals.

4. At the parish level, review whether the emotional and spiritual needs of recently bereaved people are being adequately met.

Prayer in support

Opening of Psalm 102

O Lord, listen to my prayer
and let my cry for help reach you.
Do not hide your face from me
in the day of my distress.
Turn your ear towards me
and answer me quickly when I call.

Literature

In Shakespeare's *The Winter's Tale* Leontes in a fit of irrational jealousy imagines his wife, Hermione, is committing adultery with his best friend, Polixenes. He comes to his senses and repents, but not before Hermione's good friend, Paulina, reports that she has died. Paulina supports the king in his grief and after years have passed invites him to view a statue of Hermione. A miraculous close hints at the supreme comfort of the resurrection.

Sacrament

In the Sacrament of the Sick, the priest calls down the Holy Spirit, the Consoler, to heal a person who is poorly, so that he/she may be cured of his/her ailment or receive strength through grace to confront future challenges.

5. Forgive offences

One of our greatest afflictions can be the memory of our having offended somebody. We can get sucked into a vortex of self-recrimination. We are unable to emerge from this unhappy situation by ourselves. When somebody forgives us for an offence which we have committed, we feel released from the guilt associated with that particular act and we also become newly aware that we can be forgiven for other things too, that, in other words, peace of mind is truly possible.

Origins in Scripture

The seven Penitential Psalms (6, 32, 38, 51, 102, 130 and 143) are a treasury which reveals the Jewish people's keen awareness of their sinfulness but also their understanding that God has forgiven them in the past and that they can be confident in petitioning him again to forgive further offences. Psalm 51, for example, opens as follows: "Have mercy on me, God, in your kindness./In your compassion blot out my offence./O wash me more and more from my guilt/and cleanse me from my sin" (*Ps* 51:1-2). The Psalmist is aware that the Lord God is kind and compassionate: he is not seeking to appease a fickle unknown deity.

Psalm 31 begins with a proclamation of joy: "Happy the man whose offence is forgiven,/whose sin is remitted./ Happy the man to whom the Lord/imputes no guilt,/ in whose spirit is no guile" (*Ps* 32:1-2). The Psalmist is obviously reflecting on his own experience. It is startling how evident it is to the psalmist that complete closure with regard to past mistakes is perfectly possible given the mercy of God whose depths cannot be sounded.

This highly developed culture of repentance, based on an assurance of God's mercy, proceeds from Israel's knowledge that God has established successive Covenants with his people to draw them back into communion with him. Their repeated failures have merely elicited from God further promises of mercy. The Prophet Ezekiel, speaking on God's behalf, declares: "But if the wicked man renounces all the sins he has committed, respects my laws and is law-abiding and honest, he will certainly live; he shall not die. All the sins he committed will be forgotten from then on; he shall live because of the integrity he has practised" (*Ez* 18:21-22).

Wisdom literature drew out the implications of our having been forgiven by God for our relationships with one another. Ben Sira, for example, writes: "Forgive your neighbour the hurt he does you and when you pray, your sins will be forgiven. If a man nurses anger against another, can he then demand compassion from the Lord?" (*Si* 28:2-3)

Example of Christ

On Calvary, Jesus reveals the full beauty of this spiritual work of mercy: "Father, forgive them; they do not know what they are doing," he says (*Lk* 23:34). This is extreme forgiveness: he is asking that wrongdoers who have not shown any kind of remorse should be forgiven. St Luke's Gospel is notable for its exploration of divine mercy. Here we have the Parable of the Prodigal Son which reveals the deep desire of the father to forgive his errant son: so intent upon mercy is the father that he sees the son while he is still a long way off and, casting aside his own dignity, runs to him to embrace him (*Lk* 15:11-32).

In both Matthew and Luke, Jesus urges his disciples to emulate this divine mercy in their dealings with each other: "'Be compassionate as your Father is compassionate. Do not judge and you will not be judged yourselves; grant pardon and you will be pardoned'" (*Lk* 6:27; 35-37). The connection between God's and our acts of mercy is underlined in the following line from the Lord's Prayer which Jesus teaches his apostles: "'And forgive us our debts, as we have forgiven those who are in debt to us'" (*Mt* 6:12). Jesus adds: "'Yes, if you forgive others their failings, your heavenly Father will forgive you yours; but if you do not forgive others, your Father will not forgive your failings either." (*Mt* 6:14-15). These quotations help us to see that Christian forgiveness is not a positive feeling that we generate within ourselves concerning somebody who has hurt us. Rather it is an act of will which expresses our resolve, in the context of God's having forgiven and freed us, not to submit once more to that imprisonment which hatred of another always entails.

Example of Christians historically

The early Church recognised that, because Christ had done away with sin by sacrificing himself (*Heb* 9:27), his disciples now found themselves living a new life of "freedom" in the Holy Spirit (*Ep* 1:7; *Col* 1:14). St Paul writes:

> "You must give up your old way of life; you must put aside your old self, which gets corrupted by following illusory desires. Your mind must be renewed by a spiritual revolution so that you can put on the new self that has been created in God's way, in the goodness and holiness of the truth. ...Be friends with one another, and kind, forgiving each other as readily as God forgave you in Christ" (*Ep* 4: 22-24; 32).

Radical forgiveness was possible because of the trans-formation which the members of the Church had undergone through grace.

The principle way the Church has communicated the mercy of God to those with burdened consciences is through public penance and the Sacrament of Reconciliation as this has developed over the centuries. In Confession, the priest, acting on behalf of Christ and of the Church, absolves the penitent. The reconciled person receives sacramental grace to begin again.

The fifth spiritual work of mercy, "Forgive offences", is clearly distinct from the sacrament. This work occurs when, very simply, one person forgives another. In both events, however, the mercy of God is brought to bear on an unhappy situation of sin, bringing release. The fact that all baptised people can be the human agents for such a dramatic divine intervention in another's life is not often remarked upon.

In recent times, a Catholic couple, Barry and Margaret Mizen, have demonstrated the power of this work of mercy through publicly forgiving the murderer of their son, Jimmy, who was killed in 2008. Margaret once said: "For me forgiveness is about not wanting revenge and not being angry…Jimmy's murder has done a lot of damage to this family and I can't let it do any more."

The nature and goodness of this work of mercy

1. It helps people to be more accepting of themselves, drawing a line under past mistakes, allowing a new beginning.

2. It prevents disputes from escalating and destroying natural communities: e.g. the family, the Church, civil society, groupings of nations.

3. It frees people from resentment, allowing them to use their energies for good purposes.

What can you do practically speaking?

1. Pray for the grace to forgive a particular wrong. Be patient with yourself if you find this difficult to do immediately. At the least, pray for those who have offended you, asking (if such is not the case) that they may recognise the need for repentance.

2. Go to the Sacrament of Reconciliation: the experience of being forgiven by God in this moment will sensitise you to the need to extend his mercy to others.

3. Seek to do good to somebody who has wronged you: in this way you will be paying back "with a blessing" and "inherit a blessing yourself" (1 P 3:9).

Prayer in support

For the forgiveness of others

Heavenly Father, whose Son, Jesus Christ, died on the cross to reconcile sinners like me to you, give me the grace to forgive those who have sinned against me, and in particular any person whom I now particularly recall. Pull up by the roots the tares of resentment in my heart so that the wheat of your charity may flourish in me. May your Holy Spirit, the Consoler, soothe the deep hurts others have caused me. Strengthen my weak faith that you, for whom nothing is impossible, may truly work this miracle within me. I ask this through the same Christ our Lord. Amen.

Literature

Fyodor Dostoevsky's nineteenth century novel *Crime and Punishment* recounts the awful murder in St Petersburg of two women by a former student, the penniless Raskolnikov. The novel follows Raskolnikov's attempts to evade justice until in the end his profound sense of guilt obliges him to confess to the police. He is sentenced to eight years' hard labour in a prison camp in Siberia and whilst there, supported by the love of Sonya, who has stood by him through everything, he experiences, for the first time, true remorse and a concomitant peace of mind born of an assurance of having been forgiven by God.

Sacrament

The Sacrament of Reconciliation has been given to us by Christ in his Church so that he may forgive us our sins, draw us more closely into communion with the Blessed Trinity and with other members of the Church and give us the grace that we need for our on-going conversion. Through this "second baptism" we rediscover our identity as children of our loving Father and are rendered newly capable of forgiving others.

6. Bear wrongs patiently

This spiritual work of mercy is closely connected to the preceding one. Often our forgiveness of another's sin will not bring a difficult situation to a close. With crystalline realism the Church enjoins us to remain charitable even when there is no immediate end in sight to current vicissitudes.

Origins in Scripture

God is presented by the prophets as the one who patiently bears the wrong of being rejected by his people. The Prophet Hosea beautifully captures the crisis within God which the Israelites' obduracy of heart provokes: "Ephraim, how could I part with you? Israel, how could I give you up? ...My heart recoils from it, my whole being trembles at the thought. I will not give reign to my fierce anger, I will not destroy Ephraim again, for I am God, not man: I am the holy One in your midst and have no wish to destroy" (*Ho* 11:8-9).

A similar dynamic is captured in the Wisdom literature. Psalm 78, for example, traces God's continuing faithfulness to his people, notwithstanding their fickleness: "Compassionately, however,/he forgave their guilt instead of killing them,/repeatedly repressing his anger/instead of rousing his full wrath,/remembering they were creatures of flesh,/a puff of wind that passes and does not return"

(*Ps* 78:38-39). We can also see God's patience operating in the Book of Job in which the eponymous hero and his companions question God's ways. Only at the very end of the Book does God intervene: "Where were you when I laid the earth's foundations? Tell me since you are so well-informed!" (*Jb* 38:2; 4) Job replies: "My words have been frivolous: what can I reply? …I have spoken once…I will not speak again" (*Jb* 40:4-5). God subsequently restores his fortunes. Here we see God firstly patiently bearing the wrong of Job's pride and then, when the moment is right, admonishing him.

Example of Christ

A moment when Christ bears wrongs patiently is when a guard slaps his face during his interrogation by Annas, the father-in-law of the high priest, Caiaphas, saying "Is that the way to answer the high priest?" Jesus replied: "If there is something wrong in what I said, point it out; but if there is no offence in it, why do you strike me?" (*Jn* 18:22-23) Jesus's words are not intended to demonstrate the absurdity of the guard's action. Rather, even in this extreme situation, Jesus is modelling charity towards those who hate him in the hope that, in time, they may come to their senses and repent of their sins. The guard may well have wondered subsequently why indeed he had struck Jesus. Perhaps he was given to irrational anger; perhaps he had an immature desire to curry favour with those who were powerful. Jesus's patience illuminates the darkness in the guard's heart.

This guard will have to meet Christ again at the end of time. Then the prisoner who appeared helpless will be revealed in his unimaginable strength as the Risen Lord. At that moment the guard will find that he is the one who is being called to account. As St Paul notes: "…all the truth about us will be brought out in the law court of Christ, and each of us will get what he deserves for the things he did, good or bad" (*2 Co* 5:10). While Christ is patient with us, therefore, that does not mean that he is indifferent to the quality of our actions.

This means that there is an urgency about our need to respond to Jesus's invitation to discipleship, an urgency which is captured by Jesus's parable of the barren fig tree. The vineyard owner urged the man who looked after the vineyard to cut down a fig tree which had produced no fruit for three years. "'Sir', the man replied, 'leave it one more year and give me time to dig round it and manure it: it may bear fruit next year; if not, then you can cut it down'" (*Lk* 13:6-9).

Example of Christians historically

The early Christians saw clearly that they were benefiting from Jesus's patience. St Peter writes: "Think of our Lord's patience as your opportunity to be saved…" (*2 Pt* 3:13-15). They also sought to emulate Jesus in his patience. St

Peter cites the case of a slave who is subject to a beating which he has not merited: the slave gains merit through "bearing it patiently". He adds: "This, in fact, is what you were called to do, because Christ suffered for you and left an example for you to follow the way he took" (1 *Pt* 2: 18-22). Jesus himself, of course, used the word "example" in another context: after he had washed his apostles' feet: "I have given you an example so that you may copy what I have done to you" (*Jn* 13:15). St Peter's words show that discipleship involves not just acts of service but also a steady acceptance of unavoidable difficulties through which we participate in Christ's Passion.

We are able to be patient because of grace. St Paul reminds the Christians in Colossae: "You are God's chosen race, his saints; he loves you, and you should be clothed in sincere compassion, in kindness and humility, gentleness and patience. Bear with one another; forgive each other as soon as a quarrel begins. The Lord has forgiven you; now you must do the same" (*Col* 3:12-13). Transformed by the Holy Spirit, the saints of Colossae have been chosen to be conduits of God's mercy to one another through the simple everyday act of living in each other's company.

St James notes the benefit of being patient for the one exercising this work of mercy. He writes that it is a "happy privilege" to suffer trials: "…you understand that your faith is only put to the test to make you patient, but patience too is to have its practical results so that you will become fully-developed, complete, with nothing missing" (*Jm* 1:2-4). Patience, which involves refraining from bad acts, helps us to grow personally so that we become, when the occasion requires it, more capable of engaging in good acts.

Religious life, which ordinarily involves living in community, has provided an ideal environment for exercising this spiritual work of mercy. Sister Jeanne Jugan (1792-1879), foundress of the Little Sisters of the Poor, practised it to an extraordinary degree: she uncomplainingly allowed herself to be side-lined by an influential and probably mentally unbalanced priest and her role in establishing the order remained unacknowledged throughout her lifetime. Just before she died, she told a newly professed sister: "People will talk to you about me, but let the matter drop. God knows all." It was more than twenty years after her death that her significance in the order was recognised.

The nature and goodness of this work of mercy

1. It is oriented to the good of the wrongdoer, allowing this person the opportunity to experience conversion.

2. The other's objectionable behaviour becomes a means of my sanctification.

3. It allows me to make amends for unrelated sins: I may be suffering undeservedly in this instance but I have done wrong to others on other occasions.

What can you do practically speaking?

1. Pray for somebody who annoys you.

2. Accept that redress is not always possible and find peace and inner freedom in that thought.

3. Channel energies which might have been expended in resentment into doing something good.

4. Identify within yourself those faults which grieve others and, for the sake of the common good, pray to God that he will release you from them.

Prayer in support

Suffering with Jesus by Francois Fénelon

O crucified Jesus, in giving me your cross give me too your spirit of love and self-abandonment; grant that I may think less of my suffering than of the happiness of suffering with you. What do I suffer that you have not suffered? Or rather what do I suffer at all, if I dare to compare myself with you? O Lord, grant that I may love you and then I shall no longer fear the cross.

Literature

In Chaucer's *The Franklin's Tale*, Dorigen, who is happily married to Arveragus in Brittany, agrees, in his absence in England, to accept, under pressure, Aurelius's suit but only on condition that he can remove all the rocks from the coast of Brittany, something which she is confident is impossible. Aurelius achieves this through magic. Dorigen, appalled, tells Arveragus on his return of what has happened and he tells her she must keep her promise however much it grieves him. Dorigen goes to Aurelius but he, upon learning of Arveragus's noble response, renounces his claims. Arveragus's patience, "an heigh vertu certeyn," affords Aurelius the opportunity to become a better man.

Sacrament

The Sacrament of Matrimony gives couples the graces which they need to bear with one another in the great adventure of their shared life. Those who participate in this "communion of life and love" are called to be mutually forgiving, to seek to become better for the sake of the other spouse and to accept in each other negative characteristics which persist notwithstanding sincere efforts to eliminate them.

7. Pray for the living and the dead

Intercessory prayer is the most helpful activity that we can engage in for others. Pope Emeritus Benedict noted: "We can be sure that there is no such thing as a superfluous or useless prayer. No prayer is lost" (*General Audience*, 12th September 2012). Our prayer is efficacious because we unite it with that of Jesus who never ceases to intercede for us with the Father (*Catechism of the Catholic Church* 2741).

Origins in Scripture

The Catechism helpfully describes how the principal figures in the Old Testament reveal the underlying dynamic of prayer, which is always a response to a first "initiative of love" on God's part (*CCC* 2567). Abraham, having become aware of God's compassion through God's appearance to him at Mamre (*Gn* 18:1-15), is then emboldened to petition God to save the people of Sodom (*CCC* 2571; *Gn* 18:16-33). God spoke to Moses "face to face, as a man speaks with his friend" (*Ex* 33:11) and in this intimacy Moses gained the strength to intercede tenaciously for his people (*CCC* 2576-77). David was the King "after God's own heart," the shepherd who prayed for his people: his prayer revealed complete confidence in God's promises (*CCC* 2579; *2 S* 7:18-29). On Mount Carmel Elijah achieved the return of the people to the faith, thanks to the intervention of God to whom he prayed: "Answer me, O Lord, answer me!" (*CCC* 2583; *1 K* 18:37)

The people for whom these figures prayed were those living on the earth at that particular period. The Jewish understanding of the resurrection was necessarily limited: it consisted merely in the idea that a just man's line would continue through his children. Later books, however, intimate that there may be such a thing as a personal resurrection. For example, in the second century BC Judas Maccabee ordered that sacrifices be offered in the Temple in Jerusalem for slain Jewish soldiers who had worn pagan amulets to expiate their sin (*2 M* 12:38-46). Also, psalms which look forward to God's rescuing of a person, such as noticeably Psalm 129 ("Out of the depths I cry to you O Lord"), are open to the deeper understanding subsequently accorded to them in the Christian tradition, namely that the Psalmist is appealing, on behalf of the whole people, to be rescued from death in a definitive way.

Example of Christ

The evangelists often mention that Christ prayed. A particularly striking moment is at the beginning of the second day of his public ministry: "In the morning, long before dawn, he got up and left the house, and went off to a lonely place and prayed there" (*Mk* 1:35). His disciples come upon him in this prayer: he is revealing to them the importance of prayer simply through engaging in it. He prays before the decisive moments of his mission, such as his Baptism, his Transfiguration and his Passion. He also prays before decisive moments in the mission of his disciples, for example, when he calls the Twelve or before Peter's confession of him as the "Christ of God" (*CCC* 2599-2600).

Jesus teaches his disciples to pray. He gives them the "fundamental Christian prayer," the Lord's Prayer (*CCC* 2759; *Mt* 6:9-13). He teaches them, through his own practice, the dispositions which are necessary for true prayer, one of which is filial boldness: "Whatever you ask in prayer, believe that you receive it, and you will" (*Mk* 11:24). He underlines the importance of faith: "all things are possible to him who believes" (*Mk* 9:23). Jesus admires the great faith of the Roman Centurion and the Canaanite woman (*Mt* 8:10; 15:28) (*CCC* 2610).

As well as teaching us how to pray, Jesus continues to pray for us. He "is living forever to intercede for all who come to God through him" (*Heb* 7:25). When we, as members of Christ's Body, the Church, pray, we enter into Jesus's eternal filial communication with his Father.

Example of Christians historically

The early Christians immediately understood the importance of prayer: they "devoted themselves to the teaching of the apostles and to the communal life, to the breaking of bread, and to the prayers" (*Ac* 2:42). St James and St Paul exhorted them to "pray at all times" (*Jm* 1:5-8; *Ep* 5:20). St Paul described how the Holy Spirit helps us in our prayers: he "expresses our plea in a way that could never be put into words" (*Rm* 8:26).

They also quickly realised that intercessory prayer, that is asking God on behalf of others, required a particular generosity of spirit. A Christian was called to look "not only to his own interests, but also to the interests of others" (*Ph* 2:4), even to the point of praying for those who did him harm. One thinks, here, for example of Stephen's prayer for those who were stoning him to death (*Ac* 7:60). The early Christians' intercessory prayer was characterised by intensity. For example, when Peter was imprisoned, "the Church prayed for him unremittingly" (*Ac* 12:5). When Paul finished addressing the elders of Ephesus, "he knelt down with them all and prayed" (*Ac* 20:36). Christian intercession knew no boundaries: it was "for everyone and especially for kings and others in authority" (*1 Tm* 2:1), for persecutors (*Rm* 12:14) and for those who rejected the gospel (*Rm* 10:1) (*CCC* 2634-2636).

Intercessory prayer also extended to those who had died. St Paul, writing to Timothy, prayed for Onesiphorus, who had been a great help to him: "May it be the Lord's will that he shall find the Lord's mercy on that Day" (*2 Tm* 1:18). In time, the Church, guided by the Holy Spirit, came to understand that many of those who had died in God's friendship were likely still to need purification before they could enter into the happiness of heaven: this became the doctrine of Purgatory. "From the beginning the Church has honoured the memory of the dead and offered prayers in suffrage for them, above all the Eucharistic sacrifice, so that, thus purified, they may attain the beatific vision of God" (*CCC* 1032).

The importance of intercessory prayer can be seen in the emergence of contemplative orders. Carmelite Sisters, for example, offer all of their prayers and sacrifices in union with Christ and the Church for the salvation of souls and the redemption of the world. They also make specific needs known in intercessory prayer and have a particular mission of praying for priests. The example of such religious helps clergy and lay people to be mindful of their own responsibilities with regard to prayer.

The nature and goodness of this work of mercy

1. It is an act both of complete selflessness and of utter faith.

2. It is the most helpful act that we can engage in for others.

3. It builds up our communion with our brothers and sisters in the Church on earth and with our deceased loved ones.

What can you do practically speaking?

1. Create a list of people who are in need and pray for them by name each day. Review the list each month.

2. When in conversation somebody mentions that he/she is struggling with a challenge assure that person that you will pray for him/her.

3. Offer a Mass intention for a deceased loved one.

4. Engage in small acts of self-sacrifice and offer these for deceased loved ones; alternatively go on a day pilgrimage to a local shrine and apply the graces of the indulgence that you receive to them.

Prayer in support

De profundis

Out of the depths I cry to you, O Lord,
Lord, hear my voice!
O let your ears be attentive
to the voice of my pleading.
If you, O Lord, should mark our guilt
Lord, who would survive?
But with you is found forgiveness:
for this we revere you.
My soul is waiting for the Lord,
I count on his word.
My soul is longing for the Lord
more than watchman for daybreak.
Let the watchman count on daybreak
and Israel on the Lord.
Because with the Lord there is mercy

and fullness of redemption,
Israel indeed he will redeem
From all its iniquity.

Literature

In Dante's *Purgatorio*, the poet has to ascend a mountain, at each level of which he is freed from an attachment to one of the seven deadly sins. The people whom he meets during his ascent implore him to pray for them so that they may be admitted to heaven. In reaching the top he experiences complete purification and stands on the border of heaven. The last lines are: "remade, as new trees are renewed when they bring forth new boughs, I was pure and prepared to climb unto the stars." Perhaps no other piece of literature better describes the benefit our prayers can confer on those who have died.

Sacrament

The Sacrament of Holy Orders gives the priest who is ordained the responsibility of praying for the living and the dead through the celebration of Mass and the recitation of the Divine Office. The solemn undertaking of the priest encourages all members of the Church to engage in intercessory prayer.